The Simple Guide to Understanding Shame in Children

What It Is, What Helps and How to Prevent Further Stress or Trauma

BETSY dE THIERRY

Illustrated by Emma Reeves

Foreword by Dr Marc Bush

Jessica Kingsley Publishers
London and Philadelphia

First published in 2019
by Jessica Kingsley Publishers
73 Collier Street
London N1 9BE, UK
and
400 Market Street, Suite 400
Philadelphia, PA 19106, USA

www.jkp.com

Library of Congress Cataloging in Publication Data
A CIP catalog record for this book is available from the Library of Congress

British Library Cataloguing in Publication Data
A CIP catalogue record for this book is available from the British Library

ISBN 978 1 78592 505 4
eISBN 978 1 78450 895 1

Printed and bound in Great Britain

CONTENTS

FOREWORD

In this simple, yet compressive, guide to shame, Betsy de Thierry provides us with a wonderfully descriptive account of how we can better understand and respond to children's experiences of shame.

Shame experiences are important for us to focus on, as many of us are too quick to misinterpret them as feelings of guilt, anxiety, regret, embarrassment or disgust. Perhaps the best explanation for this is that we would all rather not have to consider our own experiences of shame, because it involves confronting the memories, beliefs and sensations that make us feel ashamed.

de Thierry eloquently describes the ways in which shame can pollute social relationships, depriving children of the contact, sense of community and relationality that protects them from poorer mental health outcomes in adulthood. This makes shame an intensely painful, but very natural emotional state, as it arises out of our human need to belong. Children believe that if they do not comply and conform they will be lost, without a community and rejected. That is why we see children who have experienced the most neglectful and abusive starts in life, frequently justifying or explaining away the behaviour of their parents or carers – they are worried that they will not survive without them. Some of these children are left with the shame of being complicit in a potentially toxic family environment for the purposes of survival.

It is additionally shameful for a child to recognize and acknowledge that the very people who brought them into the world and were meant to care for them, didn't. AND that (in a shame-filled way) they think that relates to who they *are* as person, or what they *did* as a child. It is therefore important to remember that for many children disclosing the experiences they are having, and asking for help in itself can be an exceptionally shame-filled experience, especially if they are not met well by an adult.

When parenting or working with children, we need to become shame-informed to build awareness of how shame works and its detrimental, or even devastating, effect on a child's development and future. de Thierry provides a practical guide to doing this, by offering insight on how best to support children to challenge feelings of badness and wrongness that arise from shame. In doing so, the later section shows how adults can encourage children to speak about shame experiences, through building calm, compassionate and empathic responses to both the behaviours children present with, and the beliefs and thoughts they express.

It is clear that expanding the horizons of emotional literacy and creative responses in children will increase their ability to make sense of and successfully navigate shame. As de Thierry argues this must be done with the intention of providing children with new ways of belonging and forms of kind and reciprocal connection, which will support them to build their own resilience, courage and self-compassion in the face of shaming situations. Reading this guide will provide an excellent insight into how we can all avoid inadvertently shaming children and create shame-resilience and healing.

Dr Marc Bush

PREFACE

How is it possible to write a book that simplifies such a profound, unpleasant and complex concept?

In this book I have included research findings from journals, guidance from books for professionals and knowledge from experienced practitioners about shame, but I have simplified and summarized their findings so that they are accessible to all. I have tried to make it easy to read and not too 'heavy' – although that's a real challenge with a subject as complex as shame. It's important to spread knowledge and awareness of shame so we can help the next generation be free from some of the challenges associated with it that are evident in significant proportions in our society today.

The first four chapters of this book explore what shame is and how it affects us; the middle four chapters look at symptoms of shame. They explore the behaviours that often result from a sense of profound shame and what helps those children. The last two chapters explain ways to heal from shame and build shame resilience.

As a psychotherapist, teacher, mum and friend, I have seen shame rear its ugly but subtle, invisible, powerful head in many ways and places: in schools, in parenting techniques, in organizations, and so many other settings. I have also seen the life-changing negative impact that shame has created within the depths of the person impacted, even when it is so often hidden behind coping mechanisms.

I was stalked and harassed for four years before an arrest was made, and in that time I was fascinated and saddened by how many people responded with shame to the assault on my personal reputation. I had threatening emails and many malicious messages along with seeing over 40 domain names bought up in my name, not being able to have access to emails in my name as they were in use by 'someone else' and finding out that malicious emails had been sent anonymously, lying about me to people I was contracted to work with. In this frightening time when I was constantly discovering new shocking cyber attacks aimed at harming my professional reputation, I noticed the shame that I had to cognitively fight because I knew I had done nothing wrong. These attacks were the result of a few people who felt shame and couldn't bear the pain and turmoil, so had to use coping mechanisms that we explore in the middle chapters. That is how I became immensely familiar with the shame that I recognized in my work in the trauma centres, both in the victims who were totally not to blame and also in those who hurt others.

Thankfully, I have also seen the relief that results when shame is recognized and named, its role in causing problems is acknowledged and understood and thus, slowly, its impact is reduced.

In this book we will explore the way shame can be experienced and how it can impact behaviour, memory, learning, emotions and relationships, with the aim of acknowledging and thereby reducing its power.

There will be examples to illustrate how shame presents in children throughout the book. I hope it will help and transform the lives of those seeking an answer to some of the complex questions they face with the children in their world.

I have added a Further Reading section with suggestions for those of you who want to dig deeper than the simple guidance offered in this book – I could have written much more, but my intention in writing this book is to convey the essentials for people who don't have the time to read the specialist research and books which are also available.

There have been deep-thinking, reflective practitioners that have gone before me, and I am grateful to these professionals who have taken time to notice human behaviours and themes and attempt to analyze them so that we can be healthier humans! In some ways I feel awkward summarizing their life's work in such a concise book, but I hope they would applaud the motivation.

I am writing to help those of you working with and/ or living with children, who are committed to seeing them develop into healthy adults with a strong sense of identity, a confident ability to reflect and an ease in feeling and articulating feelings.

Children are only able to flourish and to develop the ability to form positive, fulfilling relationships – to be the best them that they can be – with these foundations. It's only if the toxicity of shame is reduced that healthy individuals and communities can be created!

Chapter 1

WHAT IS SHAME?

Shame is an intensely painful experience.

It is that feeling of extreme embarrassment or humiliation, coupled with sudden uncontrollable body responses which might involve feeling sweaty, dizzy, sick or tight-chested. Shame can cause you to blush, stare, laugh or become silent whilst internally it can make you want to run, hide, or be swallowed up into the ground.

Whilst this experience is an immediate reaction, its impact can last a long time if immediate relief is not found. If you experience deep shame, it can lead to reliance upon others to help you to feel normal, cared for and accepted.

There are different degrees of shame. When shame is used as a strategy by adults to force children to conform, be silent or co-operate in things that are frightening, it can lead to severe, ongoing feelings of shame.

Some common ways that shame can be triggered in children include when they:

- have to keep a secret that worries them
- have no one to play with and they are teased and called names

- have to leave a group/club/activity because they are not 'good enough'
- wear the wrong outfit to a party or event and feel stupid
- can't tell anyone what their home is really like because they are embarrassed
- need help but don't know how to ask and so are left feeling stupid
- try hard but fail at a task and they are mocked or told to try harder
- are blamed for 'asking for it' by an adult who had done something horrid to them

and other types of similar experiences.

There is increasing understanding of the way that shame can cause long-term feelings of inner turmoil and thoughts of 'not being good enough' which can limit a child's creativity and their confidence to take risks. Shame can pollute relationships because children can feel fearful about experiencing further shame and so, rather than develop healthy relationships, they can withdraw, struggle with anxiety, or fail to recognize controlling behaviours in friendships or can display controlling behaviours themselves.

When we understand shame and can identify its power in situations, we can dilute its negative impact and enable children to grow to live fulfilling lives; we can enable them to avoid internal conflict and the need to develop destructive coping mechanisms.

When shame is experienced, it functions as an urgent signal that danger is here: the danger of rejection, failure, exposure and abandonment. It is an experience rooted in interpersonal relationships. It threatens the very basic human experience of being alive and needing to belong, be loved and be accepted.

The following people have approached the subject of shame within the framework of formal, academic study and have formed different but complementary ideas about what shame is.

Louis Cozolino PhD is a professor of psychology at Pepperdine University and a private practitioner. He says that: 'core shame…is an instinctual judgement about the self and it results in a sense of worthlessness, a fear of being found out and a desperate striving for perfection' (2016, p.10).

Kaufman Kaufman was an associate professor in the counselling centre at Michigan State University and is the author of many books and academic papers on shame. He describes shame as an inner experience: 'To feel shame is to feel seen in a painfully diminished sense. The self feels exposed both to itself and to anyone else present' (1980, p.9).

Brené Brown is a number one New York Times bestselling author and a research professor at the University of Houston Graduate College of Social Work. Her TED talk is one of the top ten most watched TED talks of all time and her primary research has been on vulnerability, shame and courage. She describes shame as the 'intensely painful feeling or experience of believing we are flawed and therefore not worthy of love and belonging' (2012, p.69).

We know that the experience of shame induces a sudden sense of fear that is instinctive and not a considered reaction. This instinctive fear seems to be coupled with a sense of panic, which is a reaction more suited to obvious danger or threat.

If a child experiences shame occasionally, they are able to recover and move on and it doesn't necessarily have a negative impact, but if they are exposed to regular experiences of shame, they can develop negative coping mechanisms which can cause significant toxic stress and have a lasting impact on their relationships, emotions, behaviour and learning. Coping mechanisms will be explored in the following chapters but could include lying, pretending, avoiding challenging situations, running away or hating themselves.

The difference between shame and guilt

Shame is different from guilt because shame is usually interpreted as 'I am bad and you think I am bad' whereas guilt is interpreted as 'I did something bad.' This thought process takes place at a subconscious level, meaning it happens internally so the person is not aware of these feelings and beliefs, although they do affect their behaviour.

Guilt means that the child can usually 'fix' the problem by apologizing for the bad thing they did. However, when a child feels that *they themselves* are bad and believes that people around them think they are too, they can feel that they are not loved and wanted because they are bad and so a feeling of rejection can begin to form. This feeling can cause terror as they simultaneously subconsciously realize that they are reliant on adults to meet their needs and rejection therefore feels like a life or death issue.

Another way of putting it would be that guilt says you *made* a mistake but shame says that you *are* a mistake. Many traumatized children live with a core sense of *being* a mistake and sadly continue to live lives trying to soothe the painful, deep subconscious feelings of fundamentally being a mistake and worthless.

Contrastingly, *guilt* can be a helpful experience that can lead to improved interpersonal skills if the person experiencing it is able to do something about the uncomfortable feeling. For example, if a child hits their friend because they want a toy and then that friend cries, it can be helpful to be able to help the child to pause and notice the crying child and point out their reaction to being hit. This can lead to guilt which can motivate the child to ask to borrow the toy in future.

Shaming

Shaming a child is usually something that takes place due to a lack of knowledge rather than intentional cruelty. Adults usually relate to children in the way that they were related to as children and, as such, often use shame to motivate a child. This is due to not understanding the long-term toxic impact of shaming a child rather than being unkind. Obviously we also have to acknowledge that there is a minority of adults who choose to shame a child in order to hurt them.

Shaming a child take the form of comments like:

- 'You're so stupid'

- 'I knew you couldn't do it – you were always dumb'

- 'It wasn't you again was it Bruce? Why does it always have to be you that causes the problems?'

- 'Will you just grow up and behave rather than try and have all the attention'

- 'You are such a cry-baby'.

Shame can also occur when an adult who has been looking after a child says to the parent in front of the child: 'I am sorry to say that your child was naughty and...'

The child is disconnected from both the adults as they talk about the behaviour as if the child is not there, which can lead to feelings of rejection, disconnection and shame. Instead of having an opportunity to reflect on whatever happened and possibly admitting any wrongdoing, feeling guilty and making amends, the child is left disempowered and disconnected. This can lead to internal confusion and shame.

Instead, if the adult explained to the parent what had happened away from the child, it would enable the parent to gently ask what had happened that caused the 'naughty' behaviour in a way that would show that they believe the best about them.

Shame can happen in lots of other different contexts and we'll explore this more in Chapter 4.

What does shame feel like?

Shame is an extraordinarily powerful, instinctive, primitive feeling and bodily experience that over-whelms a person. People who experience shame will instinctively find ways of avoiding the intensity of this feeling.

Cozolino (2006) describes it as the 'visceral experience of being shunned and expelled from social connectedness' (p.234). It is an experience that is beyond words, a heightened self-conscious state where the person usually wants to run away, hide and not be seen. It triggers subconscious fears which can cause a rapid escalation of emotions to be experienced.

Herman (2011) says that shame involves:

> an initial shock and flooding with painful emotion. Shame is a relatively wordless state in which speech and thought are inhibited. It is also an acutely self-conscious state, the person feels small, ridiculous and exposed. There is a wish to hide characteristically expressed by covering the face with the hands. (p.263)

Many of us can vividly remember a situation in which we experienced shame and it may have been a defining moment for us. Other people may be able to identify symptoms of shame, but are unable to call up specific memories; this can indicate that shame is present, but has been suppressed as a coping mechanism.

Children will rarely know or use the word shame, but will recognize the experience of extreme embarrassment where they felt painful bodily reactions and they wanted to hide. These painful bodily reactions include a constricted chest, shallow breathing, dizziness, feeling sick, having an urge to wet themselves, sweaty palms or other ways that the body copes with stress.

When a child experiences shame but is then able to feel comforted rather than judged in the midst of their turmoil, they may gradually be able to talk about what happened and reflect and make sense of it. When this occurs there will probably be little negative impact of the shameful experience and it may lead to strength and growth.

If the caring adult isn't able to comfort them or is the one causing the shame, the child can experience significant fear, stress and anxiety about their worth, their sense of belonging and acceptance. This can lead to harmful coping mechanisms and a sense of deep, enduring fear.

Sophie was at her friend's house when she dropped her cup of squash on the floor and panicked and froze. Thankfully, as she stared at the spilt drink and the wet carpet and felt hot, dizzy and sick, her friend's mum soothed her with a gentle tone of voice, saying, 'It's OK sweetie. We all spill things. We know it was a mistake! Shall we clear it up now?' Immediately, the dizzy, hot, sick feelings began to lessen as she slowly looked up at her friend's mum and saw her kind eyes and then she was able to cry and be comforted. The mum was able to soothe Sophie from the pain of shame and enable a positive, nurturing experience to be added to her understanding of the world.

_____

Shame exists on a continuum

People have different experiences of shame and it's important to acknowledge the different levels of the severity of their experience so that the language we use around the issue is helpful and not over-simplified. These categories are ones I have developed – they're not diagnostic labels, but help to express the different types of shame and I've found them helpful to use in my work.

Type I

In the example of Sophie above, she experiences a short burst of shame which is painful but passes – we might describe this as a 'normal' rather than 'toxic' degree of shame. Afterwards the experience will have stayed in her conscious memory, but she's able to overcome the unpleasant feelings relatively soon after the event and can 'shake them off'.

When we experience shame, we'll often aim to avoid any repeat of the same discomfort in future – this endeavour is often a very conscious and cognitive one. This could be described as 'normal' shame.

Type II

Other children experience a deep sense of shame in their early years either because they live in abusive, neglectful, volatile homes, or if their parents lack knowledge regarding children's emotional needs.

Often, people do not consciously remember very early experiences of shame, but they are remembered on a subconscious level and carried as a deep anxiety about being abandoned, rejected and not good enough. The child will feel like they need to cover up any vulnerabilities which may expose their imperfections.

This can lead to different symptoms or coping mechanisms, such as withdrawing, lying or being a perfectionist, which will be explored in the middle sections of the book. This 'Type II' shame involves experiences and symptoms which are unhealthy, and can cause shame symptoms in behaviour, emotions, relationships and life choices.

———————

James was a talented football player and loved playing matches on Saturdays. One day he was getting ready for school when his parents started arguing badly and it became so violent that he started to get scared that one of them would die. James ended up running to his school field for his match because he didn't want to be late, but once the game started, he couldn't quite concentrate because he was feeling so anxious. During the game James kicked an amazing shot but unfortunately it was into his team's own goal. His team mates shouted and yelled while he stood frozen to the spot. He felt sick and almost wet himself and ran off the pitch. He didn't want to talk to anyone and wanted to disappear. When the coach found him and tried to reassure him, James said he was feeling sick because his dog was poorly. He felt shame about the goal and about his parents and his feelings of anxiety but didn't know what to say or how to explain all the confusion he felt. He felt that he couldn't mention his parents and the real reason for his anxiety because he felt like it was probably his fault that they were arguing. He felt shame. It wasn't his fault at all, but he felt the weight of shame about an experience that was both secret and frightening to him.

_____

Type III

Sadly there are other children who experience early shame which is very painful, perhaps because of the degree of secrecy or terror they experience or how sensitive they are to it.

These children adopt similar mechanisms that work hard at avoiding shame. However, the shame also poisons their sense of identity because of the severity or duration of their experience. The feeling of shame becomes embedded in their everyday life as a heavyweight and implicit secret feeling that we would call a 'core sense of shame'.

The complexity of the coping mechanisms that they adopt to protect their sense of shame usually become enmeshed with their identity and hard to separate. I call these shame experiences and symptoms Type III.

The difference between Type II and Type III shame is marked by the length of time and degree of humiliation and fear experienced, which is greater in Type III. The more frightened, humiliated, unprotected and undefended a child feels, the further down they have to push the unbearable, horrific feelings into the subconscious. The deeper these negative feelings are pushed, the further from conscious awareness, the harder they are to reflect on or make sense of, and the more poisonous they become to our psyche.

When Charlotte was born she was desperately wanted but her mum wasn't able to be all that she wanted to be. Her mum was struggling with mental health challenges and every cry that Charlotte made sent her into a panic as she tried, but wasn't able, to meet her needs. This led to Charlotte having to spend long periods of time on her own with little emotional interaction with anyone else. She grew up fearful of people and nervous about causing problems or being 'in the way'. She soon learned that when she made people happy they were kind to her and so she smiled and danced and people thought she was happy all the time.

Inside Charlotte was developing a strong sense that she was only wanted when she made people happy and so when family friends came to stay and asked her to do things she felt uncomfortable about, she said yes, 'as long as it made them happy'. After these scary things happened and the family friends were happy with her, she felt all sorts of other strong feelings of terror, powerlessness and confusion, but she pushed those down too so that she could be loved by being happy and smiley.

Charlotte was known to 'be off with the fairies' but people thought that was quite cute. Actually she would choose to wonder off into her made-up world in her mind where she was less powerless and scared and she had make-believe close friends and adults who took care of her. Her time spent in this fantasy world increased and her time spent with friends in her class lessened and she was known as someone who was a 'loner'.

When Charlotte went to take her ballet exam, the teacher shouted at her as she walked in and so she wet herself. She didn't cry, she just laughed because she immediately went off to her special made-up land in her mind to avoid the shame. But the shame left its poisonous mark, as she was shouted at all the way home by her dad. She continued to battle with her everyday life, with making friends or being pleased with anything she did because deep down she felt unwanted, never good enough and scared of making mistakes where people would 'find out' that she was actually a person with real needs.

_____

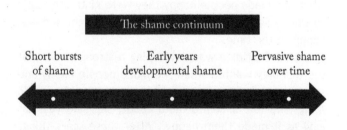

Figure 1.1 The shame continuum

Overcoming shame

Shame is as central to the human experience as anxiety or suffering, but far more difficult to identify due to the complex entanglement of feelings, bodily responses and coping mechanisms that hide it. As a result, it is frequently misunderstood and the impact of it is rarely acknowledged.

The paradox about shame is that there is shame about shame!

Most people don't want to think about shame, and yet when we do, we can learn from the experience, dilute its negative impact and grow in healthy relationships and emotions.

Shame hates being spoken about: as people grow in courage to speak about and be vulnerable about their intense experience of shame, they can learn to break the power it has over their own lives.

Simply demanding that children stop feeling shame does not work and, ironically, can increase the experience of shame and therefore can cause an escalation of the shame symptoms. However, you can help a child to overcome feelings of shame by finding ways to enable them to talk about the feeling in their body and the emotions that accompany them, whilst ensuring that they experience a warm and empathetic response from a caring adult. When this happens, the fear of being rejected immediately ceases.

When a child is able to courageously explore the physical and emotional symptoms of shame that impact on their behaviour, emotions, relationships and learning, shame's toxicity is minimalized.

But, when shame is not appropriately recognized, the impact can grow and the child can move along the continuum into more complex shame (Type II or Type III). The toxicity increases, even if it is not evident externally, because the feeling resides deep in the subconscious.

If an adult is able to comment themselves when they experience shame or see others wincing in shame on a TV show or in a book, the child will be better equipped to understand these difficult feelings, grow up recognizing the experience and be able to speak about it with more confidence. In this way, learning to identify shame, and understanding how to break its power in our own lives through reflection, exploration, empathy and compassion, can help to heal it in the lives of the children we are seeking to help.

Going back to the example above, if, when James kicked the football into the wrong goal, an adult was able to say 'James, I am wondering if you feel really bad inside and maybe so embarrassed that you may have wanted to hide or run away?' to which James may nod or shrug his shoulders. The adult could continue, 'When I feel that sometimes it can feel like it's all useless and I'm stupid, but actually that's just because I feel confused inside about why I did something silly. But we all do things we don't mean to, don't we?' and James may shrug but look less in turmoil. The adult could continue, 'When I was nine years old I swam a length in a race and thought I had won but when I got out of the pool I realized I had swum across the other swimmers' paths. I felt so bad. My face went red and I thought I was going to be sick. It took a while before I realized that I felt like I had failed everyone.' At that point, James may say, 'That's what I felt like.' He may not be able to speak about the worries he has about his parents yet, but if that adult is able to chat often he may begin to feel safe enough to tell him these worries.

Social attitudes to shame

I see shaming behaviours in schools and in families, including socially accepted methods for disciplining children such as telling them to grow up or act like a friend or a neighbour's child.

In some ways it's helpful to compare public awareness of shame to awareness of sugary snacks. In years gone by, sugary snacks were considered appropriate for children but nowadays there is growing awareness of the lasting harm they can cause.

Many people haven't yet been made aware of the negative impact and consequences of such a deeply painful method of encouraging conformity, which is why it's important to spread the message that shame will never elicit positive emotions and outcomes – it will only cause the child who experiences it to create methods of coping which are mostly counter-productive, subconscious and toxic.

We need to speak up about the subject so that we can create families, schools, organizations and communities in which vulnerability, empathy, kindness and compassion are normal

Reflection points

- Did you experience shame as a child? What did it feel like? Did it have an impact on your own life?

- Can you think of a time when you might have shamed a child, even if unintentionally?

- Can you think of ways in which children could be shamed in school or community settings?

Chapter 2

THE IMPACT OF SHAME

Humans need to belong

Shame is a painful but natural human emotion.

We're born with the knowledge that we are vulnerable and our lives are dependent on other humans to help us to survive.

As a result, we carry a deeply held instinct that it's a necessity to be accepted by our tribe because we have a deep need to belong and to connect with others.

When a child is guided through the experience of shame by attentive, emotionally connected caregivers who are able to speak about and help the child process the experience with comfort, empathy and kindness, it can be read as a sign that the child and adult are both human and are both interdependent – the adult is confirming that the child really does belong and is accepted. As a result, the shame does not become toxic.

'Toxic shame' occurs in Types II and III shame (introduced in the previous chapter), where a child feels a powerful unspoken, subconscious fear that their needs won't be met and that they will be abandoned, rejected and left alone with no 'tribe'. This causes intense and painful emotional and physiological reactions. Shame is not just a feeling but also a profound experience affecting our physiological systems, identity, emotions and relationships.

In *Counselling Skills for Working with Shame* (2015), counselling psychologist and trauma expert Christiane Sanderson writes about the long-term impact of the experience:

> Over time the pervasive nature of chronic or toxic shame and the accompanying intense and overwhelming feelings lead to the belief that the core self is defective, inadequate and unacceptable to others. For some people, these negative self-beliefs can become so corrosive that they infect the very being of the person with the sense that they are irredeemably flawed and therefore unworthy of love or being alive. (p.24)

So, while shame is a perfectly natural human emotion, it also has potential to be the most destructive of human emotions. It can damage a person's image of themselves in ways that no other emotion can, causing a person to feel deeply flawed, isolated, inferior, worthless and unlovable.

The body's response to shame

As mentioned in Chapter 1, when a person feels shame, it is a sudden, powerful sense of panic, fear and shock, which can often cause them to blush or feel faint or sick. They may have heart palpitations, perspire, become dizzy or have ringing in their ears. Usually the person wants to flee but if that's not possible they may cover their face with their hands, look downwards or stare in a state of frozen fear. As these physical things are happening, and of course everyone is different in what they experience, their threat response is stimulated. You may have heard of something called the 'fight, flight or freeze' response, which is also referred to as the 'threat response'. It is based in our brainstem, which is the area of the brain near the back of the neck. This is where our most basic responses like breathing and heart rate are based. In fact, it's the only area of the brain that is fully formed when a baby is born. This area is linked to another area in the brain called the 'limbic system', which, when faced with something it identifies as a threat, makes our emotions respond with panic. This releases hormones to prepare and enable our bodies to run (flight), hide (freeze) or scream loudly or physically fight (fight).

Meanwhile, when this threat response happens, the ability to think, be rational, negotiate or reflect goes 'offline'. The rational part of the brain is the front part and is called the 'prefrontal cortex'. So when a person is faced with threat, or what their subconscious thinks is threat, their brainstem responds with a survival threat response (fight, flight or freeze) and causes the emotional brain – the limbic system – to release hormones ready for action. This means that the primary neural activity is in a survival response leaving very little movement to be in the prefrontal cortex.

A part of this emotional brain – the amygdala – sets the whole brain into a panic alarm response system. I tell the children I work with that it's as if the brainstem catches fire due to threat and the limbic brain has a smoke alarm (the amygdala) that has been set off which makes a huge disruptive noise to make sure there is an appropriate response to the threat!

The other area of the brain that goes 'offline' when this threat response is activated is the Brocas' area, which is responsible for speech and language. That's why it can be really difficult to express how we feel in words when we've just experienced something really awful.

This is also why, when a person has experienced shame, they can't usually reflect or speak about it straight away. They need to calm down and recover from the shock of the experience before they can reflect on what happened and talk about it. Then they can only reflect or talk with adults that they feel emotionally safe with.

Problems caused by coping mechanisms

Limited self-awareness and ability to reflect

When a child experiences repeated shame, the brain is clever at creating coping mechanisms to dull the sense of pain. But these coping mechanisms can inhibit the child's ability to reflect. Being able to reflect is reliant on the prefrontal cortex, or the 'thinking brain'. But when the person is exposed to continual threat or shame, that part of the brain goes 'offline' and instead instinctual defensive behaviour takes charge. It can take a while for the person to feel calm and safe after experiencing threat or perceived threat, and some children rarely reach this state. Thus, the brain can be stuck in a place where reflection is almost impossible due to feeling unsafe. When a person cannot reflect easily, they are unable to develop self-awareness, which is an essential aspect of the development of a healthy identity.

> [Shame] perhaps more than any other emotion is intimately tied to the physiological expression of the stress response… This underscores…the function of shame as an arousal blocker. Shame reduces self-exposure or self exploration. (Schore 2003, p.154)

Negative core beliefs

Shame is a very intense physiological response, which can be accompanied with strong negative cognitions such as:

- 'I am a loser'

- 'I am an idiot'

- 'I knew I was stupid'

- 'I knew I was unlovable'.

When a child hears from the people around them, 'you are stupid', 'you cause me so much trouble', 'it was easier before you were around', 'you are a troublemaker', the child eventually comes to believe those things about him or herself. These words become enmeshed internally with the experience of rejection and the shame that they are not good enough.

There are many possible negative core beliefs that can be powerful: for example, 'it's not safe to be happy' if when a child is happy they are told off for not being thoughtful enough; or, if a child is often shouted at for needing the toilet at an inconvenient time, they can internalize core belief that it's not safe to have needs.

_____

Richard was on a camp when he developed a urine infection. He was in pain and had to be taken to the hospital in the night and given antibiotics. For several days he was on his own feeling ill. When he arrived back home he was greeted by his father who said in a stern voice, 'We'll have to take you to the doctors, won't we.' The cross face, lack of empathy and sternness led to Richard feeling that he wasn't normal and that there was something wrong with him, and he felt isolated, alone and scared.

_____

Limited vulnerability and creativity

When a child is made to feel like an inconvenience, is rejected or is told that they are not as good as their friends and peers, they can become fearful of rejection and failure. The fear that takes a hold in their subconscious impacts their ability to be vulnerable and share who they really are with others. This in turn can hinder their relationships and their ability to take risks and create. There is more about how a child may respond to protect their vulnerability in Chapters 5–8.

Creativity demands that the child takes a risk as there is a chance that their creation may not turn out how they'd like it to. Failure is an essential part of the normal creative process and creativity enables people to express themselves and lets others see what they enjoy and love. This is tough to do when the child's mind is full of negative core beliefs and a fear of rejection and vulnerability. Brené Brown believes that shame can crush our ability to create and emotionally connect to others:

> Shame breeds fear. It crushes our tolerance for vulnerability, thereby killing engagement, innovation, creativity, productivity, and trust. And worst of all, if we don't know what we are looking for, shame can ravage our organizations before we see any outward sign of a problem. Shame works like termites in a house. It's hidden in the dark behind the walls and constantly eating away at our infrastructure, until one day the stairs crumble. (Brown 2012, p.189)

Creating crippling need to compare

With the excitement, relief and thrill of a new birth, the parent is usually relieved to hear the profound words 'Your child looks normal. Everything looks fine.'

However, it doesn't take long for the parents to be nervous about normal, and instead feel compelled to compare their precious new life to other babies, either in real life or even on social media! Parents can feel anxious if their baby isn't reaching the milestones at the same time as other babies and and they can unwittingly put pressure on the tiny things to learn new skills to reduce the feelings of shame deep within the parents' subconscious. This is how shame can be a part of a baby's early life experience. It can be experienced in their parents' anxious eyes, in the atmosphere of the room where parents compare their offspring, and in the pleading for them to learn a skill that they are not quite ready for.

Children soon learn that they will be compared with others: their looks, speed at learning new skills, social skills, academic learning and everything else. They can also quickly learn that they just aren't good enough. This can cause the very foundation stones of their identity to be formed entrenched in feelings of shame and failure.

Another common reason for feelings of shame for children as they grow up is failing to fulfil the roles they are expected to. In particular, those who do not conform to the traditional ways children of their gender are expected to look and act can also often be made to feel ashamed for being different. Psychologist Christiane Sanderson (2015) speaks of the long-term impact of the expectation from parents: 'roles are expected patterns of behaviour imposed by others, usually in early childhood, which become life scripts' (p.76).

Inability to relate to or connect with others

When a person has experienced toxic shame it causes a profound ripple effect in all relationships. We will be exploring the ways that children (and adults) can defend themselves and cope with the extremely frightening feelings of shame in Chapters 5–8.

Ultimately, the pain of shame, the fear of rejection and abandonment and the sense of being a bad mistake are too much for anyone to live with in their conscious day-to-day life and so the brain works out how to avoid the feelings. Some children withdraw and avoid emotionally connecting with others. Others deny who they really feel that they are and create a 'better' more easily accepted version of themselves to offer to the world. Others become angry, defensive and critical; this can either be internalized so they present as emotionally calm, or they may act out those feelings and be known as people who are angry and critical. Then there are the tools to protect themselves from others, such as the use of projection (so they are never wrong!), blaming others (similar!) or they may self-blame, hate themselves and sabotage themselves – sometimes through self-harm – to punish themselves for being so 'useless' and unwanted.

All of this does not take place at a cognitive level, but is a subconscious response to feeling the terror of toxic shame.

Chapter 10 will explore ways to create shame resilience.

Sam was always told that he needed to try harder because he was not as good at school as his cousins. Every day someone would sigh and say, 'Flip me, do you think your cousin John would do/say or act like that? Will you just be more like him?' He grew up trying to be more like his cousins but he continually felt like he was a failure and never good enough. He longed to be accepted for who he really was, a person very different to his cousin John, but very gifted and unique and brilliant. He struggled with depression in adulthood and never felt good enough to try for promotions or to ask anyone out.

Reflection points

- Ask yourself 'What is it that I don't want this child to see of me?' and 'What is it that this child is fearful of me seeing in them?'

- Do you feel like the child you are caring for has a sense of belonging?

- How can you see where shame limits creativity, risk-taking and connection?

Chapter 3

THE NEUROSCIENCE OF SHAME

The threat response — digging deeper

Each and every child is unique and how each child responds to shame is also unique. Some children seem to be more sensitive to it than others. What we do know, however, is that shame is intrinsically linked to the threat response, as explained in Chapter 2.

Let's look at an example of the threat response in action. Let's think about Sarah, who has the worst spelling results in the class. The teacher gets everyone's attention and she tells them how badly Sarah has done. The teacher may be aiming to motivate Sarah by comparing her to the rest of the class, but shame is never good at motivating. The critical point for Sarah is not the result of the spelling test but the powerful bodily feelings that occur immediately as a response to the experience of shame. The bodily response happens so quickly that Sarah didn't have a chance to decide that she didn't care about the spelling test because her body responded as if it mattered. Maybe Sarah immediately almost wet herself? Or maybe she started to faint? Or did she freeze and stare like a scared rabbit in headlights? Did she laugh awkwardly? Did she run?

Did she feel sick? She probably felt at least some of these bodily sensations.

The involuntary body response, accompanied by strong feelings and negative thoughts, will be what she will remember, maybe in her subconscious rather than in her easily accessible memory, and will be what motivates her either not to even try in the next test, or to work hard to be perfect, or to cheat, or to stay off school, or to pretend to be ill, or anything else that might help her to avoid feeling that shame again. If the child can't avoid experiencing shame and they are frequently shamed, they can develop a prolonged sense of shame, which can reduce levels of endorphins and dopamine (feel-good hormones) and increase cortisol and noradrenalin (stress hormones).

When this initial physical involuntary threat response is activated, the child will struggle to speak, think or process. The child's body then responds to protect itself with the release of cortisol and adrenaline to enable them to fight or flee. This can make the child suddenly full of energy, fidgety, agitated, aggressive or disruptive. They may giggle, joke, run or act in other ways that release the energy from their body. It also results in the child struggling to answer questions regarding their behaviour or to think about the consequences of it. Obviously in a lot of environments, this can lead to being told off or, worse still, further shaming. What they really need is an adult to come quickly alongside them and offer empathy; not pity, because that can increase the shame, but kind, nurturing care that seems protective to their vulnerability. Having an adult to help the child process the frightening experience can enable the shame to remain in the conscious memory and stops it becoming toxic.

Children who regularly feel shame and the subsequent powerful threat response can spend the rest of their lives trying to protect themselves from another such experience by building a set of subconscious protective mechanisms.

Shame in toddlers

It can be helpful to look at how a toddler's brain begins to experience shame and how that can impact their development. A toddler's world is changing rapidly. As they become more mobile, their primary caregivers are no longer as intimately attuned to their movements and they are more exposed to danger (such as falling and hurting themselves). They experience the occasional 'No!' from their primary caregiver and they have to navigate through the shock and stress of what seems to be a rupture in the consistent love and care from them. Of course, this rupture and repair is helpful for the child to grow and even the accompanying short burst of cortisol (stress hormone) that is released can be helpful for brain growth and development. When the primary caregiver looks at a toddler with a disapproving glare to stop dangerous behaviour and says, 'No! Don't try and drink mummy's coffee, darling', the response is: 'a sudden lurch from sympathetic

arousal to parasympathetic arousal, creating the effects
we experience in shame – a sudden drop in blood
pressure and shallow breathing' (Gerhardt 2004, p.49).
It seems that a healthy dose of cortisol is helpful, but an
unhealthy dose is potentially toxic. For the toddler in
our example, if the glare remains, the physiological and
emotional response may become damaging, but if the
adult's face becomes kind and calming, the cortisol dose
can be helpful for developing maturity and the rupture
and repair can make the relationship stronger and the
world safer.

When you can't fight or flee

When a child is shamed and they feel frightened,
they assess the situation in milliseconds, and if they
are unable to fight or run because the person is big
or loud or scary, then the only option that remains is
to freeze. When a child is abused, either physically
or sexually, they usually can't run away or fight so
they have to freeze in order to stay alive. Significant
trauma such as abuse causes deep shame and complex
survival strategies to be adopted in the subconscious.
Dissociation is the most complex response; the body
could freeze or shut down momentarily or the response
could be more serious and the person could dissociate
to many different degrees. Ultimately this response
ends up being a coping mechanism for someone who
feels that disappearing is the only option to stay alive.
The other problem is that, if the child frequently feels

unable to fight or flee and they have no choice but to freeze, it becomes the instinctive response to any form of fear. So when their body gets challenged with feelings or sensations they can't tolerate, they try and disappear. This can lead into complex dissociative responses which can be hindering to a child's life unless they find an adult who can comfort them, support them and help them out of the state of fear paralysis which is probably well hidden from casual observers.

Dissociation – the overwhelm response

Dissociation is a coping mechanism that can occur when a child is in overwhelm and has run out of coping resources due to too much trauma and shame. Mild dissociation is a natural response to continual overstimulation or repeated shock or fear, but the person can quickly control the glazing over and daydreaming state and is aware of it. Moderate dissociation becomes problematic because it becomes an instinctive response to overwhelm that can interrupt daily life. It is a clever, but painful, method of splitting off an aspect that is too much to cope with.

The child may need to split off from the fear, terror and painful feelings. But this dissociation also cuts them off from more positive feelings, such as happiness and pleasure. They may split off or shut down uncomfortable sensations so that they can't feel the painful reminders of the bodily pain that they felt terrified by. However, that can mean that they also are not easily aware of other bodily sensations, such as hunger or needing the toilet.

They could split off the memories of a specific period of time so that they don't have to remember them in their present life. However, even if they do not have conscious memories of that time, their body may still remember the difficult sensations they felt, and this can lead to feelings of confusion about the chunks of their life that seem to be missing from their memories.

Describing the complex survival tool of dissociation, Silberg (2013) quotes a girl who was forced to visit her father who had abused her: 'My face is smiling but my brain is crying…' (p.196).

Dissociation is able to anaesthetize the person's pain and enable them to carry on with their daily life. However, the internal 'weight' of the dissociative fear, shame and overwhelm can be exhausting and troublesome. Dissociation also enables the child to continue to relate to their primary caregiver even if they are abusive or frightening, because they have split off those memories so that they can have their basic needs met. Sanderson (2015) says that 'dissociation allows the child to remain blind to betrayal by significant others especially in the face of repeated shame, humiliation and abuse' (p.43).

A bitter irony is that a child, young person or an adult can experience a great deal of shame for not speaking out, fighting or running when an adult frightened or hurt them. They desperately need to have the opportunity to hear how the primitive survival functions enabled them to survive situations that were too much for them to cope with. We should always approach dissociation with a sense of awe, respect and empathy for what the person has endured that led them to having to create in their subconscious such a complex and problematic response.

Shame as a tool to stay safe

Although we would all rather that children never experienced feelings of terror and powerlessness, if they do, it seems that shame does sometimes have a purpose in protecting the child from life-threatening danger. Allan Schore (2003) writes about the helpful way that shame enables the child to stay physically safe due to immobilization. It can be helpful to downregulate, or stop the child from having a loud emotionally demonstrative response such as screaming or fighting, when that would escalate the threat. In unsafe environments, it can stop the child fighting for survival and thus becoming physically exhausted and in danger. Instead, they become emotionally and psychologically exhausted by internalizing feelings of shame, but manage to survive and stay alive.

> Shame signals (e.g., head down, gaze avoidance, and hiding) are generally registered as submissive and appeasing, designed to de-escalate and/or escape from conflicts. Thus, insofar as shame is related to submissiveness and appeasement behavior, it is a damage limitation strategy, adopted when continuing in a shameless, non submissive way

might provoke very serious attacks or rejections.
(Andrews and Gilbert 1998, p.102)

The problem with trying to remember or talk about past shame experiences

Thinking about the brain in terms of two hemispheres can be a helpful way to understand some very simplified concepts about memory and shame. We understand that there is a left and a right hemisphere and our brain stores implicit, non-verbal memory of emotions and experiences in the right hemisphere of the brain. When we can quickly process and make sense of our negative experiences using our left brain, any toxic impact is minimalized. The right hemisphere stores sensory experiences collected and mixed up all together, and the role of the left brain is to sort and file the experiences so that they don't negatively impact our behaviour without cognitive choice and understanding. The brain does that by reflecting, talking, playing and making sense of the experience.

When a child experiences shame, the right brain stores it as a physical sensation and strong emotions. If the shock and fear are too overwhelming, and there isn't a caring, empathetic adult to help process the shock, then the emotions, physical sensations and any accompanying negative thoughts and interpersonal experiences become separated and are stored in the subconscious. So it can be hard to remember when we were shamed and how we responded if we were really scared or shocked.

The impact of toxic shame can be minimalized when an adult is empathetic and kind

A young child needs their primary caregivers to consistently help them feel comforted and reassured if they feel embarrassment or shame. By doing this they are enabling the brain to have a response that is familiar and comforting when they feel any shock, fear and shame. This will enable them to have resilience against the toxic shame that can be like a poison in our subconscious. There is an exploration of this in Chapters 9 and 10.

Sandra was told off in class all week long. No one knew that at home things were really tough and she had been confused by what her cousin had asked her to do to him. In assembly they had the star of the week and clapped those who had succeeded. Then they made the children who had been on the red traffic light for bad behaviour stand up while everyone looked at them. In that moment Sandra wanted to shout, 'But you don't understand, I've been scared and worried...'. Her mouth locked tight, she felt dizzy and she stood there without feeling her body. It was like she wasn't really there. From that point on she has struggled to explain what's going on and why she sometimes feels sad. It's like her mouth is still locked up. She felt like she was stupid and made bad things happen.

Reflection points

- Where have you felt shame in your body?
- Have you seen children responding to shame?
- Can you name some ways they have responded?

Chapter 4

SOURCES OF SHAME

Shame is experienced in many different contexts. Sometimes children experience shame simply because they are human and shame happens. Sometimes shame becomes deeply rooted in a person when they experienced things as a child that left them fearful for their survival, often due to parents not realizing the devastating impact of small but powerful interactions that leave a toxic trail. Sometimes shame is used to force a child to conform and submit. Shame may have quick results for the parent because the child does what the adult wants, but sadly the turmoil the child experiences in those moments can springboard on to create negative coping mechanisms that are deeply entrenched in their day-to-day life.

No child is born experiencing shame but it is believed that shame can be experienced from around 15 months of age. Such early experiences can be stored in a child's preverbal, right brain sensory memories, but without an accompanying story to help them make sense of the powerful subconscious feeling. This can create insecurity, as the child can carry a deep sense of discomfort but with no cognitive understanding to make sense of it.

Parenting techniques

Shame and fear used to force a child to obey

There are two ways to quickly force a child to obey and they are fear and shame. Negotiating and listening to a child can be exhausting. It demands emotional energy from the adult and therefore can be challenging to those who are already struggling with their daily life. This can lead to parents sometimes using shame or fear to force children to obey.

When a child has had a primary caregiver who has soothed, calmed and helped to regulate their emotions, responses and reactions, they are being co-regulated. A child needs the experience of co-regulation before they can self-regulate. The voice of the adult(s) who helped them be calm and comforted by co-regulating with them becomes like an internal voice that enables them to do exactly what they would have done with that safe adult when they were small. Experiencing co-regulation with a primary caregiver is important for healthy brain development. The adults need to be self-regulated themselves to co-regulate and therefore help a child learn self-regulation, but they also need to be regulated in the face of a child's challenging behaviour rather than feel powerless and angry and react in an unhelpful way. When a parent is overwhelmed themselves, and feels powerless about their child's behaviour, they can need to take power quickly so that they feel control and therefore can use fear or shame to make the child submit. However, when a child is shamed they may obey quickly, but whatever way they instinctively respond to the big painful feelings will potentially become their instinctive response for the rest of their life.

Early eye contact with adults

When a baby looks into the eyes of their primary caregiver and sees anger or frustration, the baby can instinctively look away to avoid further rejection. Obviously if the primary caregiver is struggling with depression, overwhelm or other challenges, they can be frustrated with the demands of the child and this can lead to the child feeling unwanted and unloveable. This can lead to the creation of procedural memory that causes them to naturally avoid looking into the eyes of others. When a child senses that they are unwanted, a burden, a disappointment, disgusting or unlovable, it becomes a burden of shame that they carry around in their subconscious without knowing the name of the tiring weight they feel (Type II–III shame).

Katherine had long hair and when she was 10 years old she decided to cut off a significant chunk by herself. She remembers that it was the night before the school photos and she was thinking that she hoped she wouldn't have to be in the photos if it went wrong. It did go wrong, which was tough because she says that she wasn't feeling very happy or confident at the time, which is probably why she did it. Her mum took her to the hairdressers to have them sort it out, but she still remembers her mum talking to the whole room of people and them laughing at her. The following day she had to be in the school photo and wished she could be invisible. She says that the incident impacted her hugely, causing her to struggle to accept herself and to struggle with feelings of anxiety.

This is shame, a painful state where she feels frightened, stupid and worthless in the very depth of her being. If Mum, in the story above, was able to quickly comfort and reassure her, then help her wonder why she did it whilst also offering to help her sort it out and protect her embarrassment from others who may comment, the impact would have been significantly reduced, if not completely nullified. How quickly the parent can repair this relational rupture determines how toxic the shame will become. Short bursts of shame which are quickly repaired by communication within a caring and nurturing relationship are a normal part of being human but the 'repair' needs to be genuine, emotionally warm and as quick as possible after the incident.

Abuse, neglect, secret family problems

Where a family hides behind a mask of being happy and healthy but where there are actually deep problems hidden, such as abuse, domestic violence, a parent with mental illness or substance abuse, shame will breed. The parents who are battling with such challenges can be supported if the family ask for help, but often there is too much shame to ask and so the secret continues and the shame grows stronger, deeper and more hidden.

When a family faces painful challenges, such as a parent with cancer or another serious illness, the family members can usually talk about it and there is usually empathy and kindness shown freely. However, when there is mental illness or substance abuse, the family often hide the challenges behind closed doors to pretend that everything is OK and shame breeds in secrecy and pretence.

When a child has established a strong enough relationship outside of the family home to be able to feel safe, they may be courageous enough to risk telling that caring adult how scared they feel and the adult may be able to get support for the family. No child should experience the secret of a dysfunctional, frightening home life without the support of other adults; no child should feel shame that causes them to become anxious and take responsibility for things that no child should have to bear. The secretive nature of this shame can cause Type II–III shame to be experienced.

Online peer pressure

Social media is continually modelling public shaming as if it is a normal and a healthy thing to do. It is a misunderstanding of the human right to have an opinion. It breeds shame-based assertions, opinions and comments as if our words hold no power and it's within our rights to shame others, despite knowing little context. Our human right to express our own opinion should have boundaries regarding not having the right to shame and criticize others. Children are growing up reading public comments which shame others in how they look, how they speak, what they say, and so the consequence is often that teenagers learn it's safer to be 'unseen' and blend in with the others because standing out could be so painful. Shame-avoidant behaviours have also become the norm of our society due to the quantity of nasty words flying around.

Being compared

As mentioned in Chapter 2, when adults compare children to each other in order to motivate them to be better at something, the child can become sad and feel shamed that they cannot do something. Comparison can cause shame and yet society seems to be driving us to compare ourselves because it seems to model comparison and shaming as normal behaviours and seems to laugh at the thought that it causes long-term emotional impact.

Parents have often been taught to use comparison to shame children in the name of discipline: 'Little Johnny never does that – why do you?' and 'If you do that again I'll tell all the neighbours.'

Teachers can often use comparison to shame children but often do not realize that the words they use are shame-based. I heard only this week of a headmaster who publicly shamed children in assembly for being naughty by getting them to stand up and listing their behaviours publicly. This would have had long-term impact on the children's emotions, relationships, learning and self-esteem.

Having your needs dismissed

When we feel that we have a need, we try to express that need, but if we are told that we shouldn't expect to have that need met, we can feel shame.

When babies and children need attention and they are mocked or shamed for that need, we are causing them to feel that there is something wrong with them. So often we hear toddlers scream in public and an adult say 'stop crying', 'boys don't cry', 'you're so annoying'. This internalized shame can sit in the core of their identity as a fear, which can be activated any time they have another need. This can lead them to want to deny their vulnerability and needs, which can lead to emotional shutdown as a way to survive.

Babies and children need to know that the need for attention and emotional connection is as basic as the need for food and drink. When they are isolated, put in 'time out' for ages, made to wait alone next to teachers' doors outside of the classroom, put in buggies facing nothing for hours 'because they are an easy baby', this can all contribute to a deep-rooted sense of rejection, unworthiness, abandonment and terror about being needy and can confirm their subconscious shame-based fears that they are a mistake and a failure. These negative experiences sit in silence in the subconscious of the child, young person or adult, creating behaviours and fears that make no sense to them.

Self-blame

It is a natural response for children to think that when bad things happen, it is their fault. Whilst we know that the child is blameless and could not have caused the nasty event, we can understand these feelings if we recognize that children find it impossible to blame their caregivers for letting them down.

Children are usually aware of their vulnerability and they have a deep, instinctive fear of abandonment to the extent that they'd rather clutch at any attachment figure, however volatile, because their survival is dependent on them and therefore it's easier to blame themselves. This means that sadly children can easily absorb the shame projected onto them, even if it's subtle. They can pick up on rejection and frustration and learn compensatory behaviours such as hiding, being good or creating a scene to get the attention or other responses that they so desperately need. We will explore this in the next chapters.

Shame used to silence victims

Sadly, we know that adults who want to harm children usually use shame to ensure that they won't be caught out. They make sure that the child will feel so disgusted that they will not be able to speak about what the adult did because they are so deeply ashamed of not saying 'no'. Yet we know that for a child to say 'no' is so difficult in such circumstances, because the speech and language centre of the brain goes offline when the threat response is activated, making talking almost impossible.

This is why it can take adults years to disclose childhood abuse, which then creates more shame because they feel stupid about their silence. Shame is used to ensure that child soldiers, or trafficked children and adults, for instance, won't escape or tell anyone. When we teach people about the power of shame, and that physical symptoms and subconscious coping mechanisms develop to avoid the dreadful experience in order to try and protect their vulnerability, they can begin to understand and they can begin the journey to free themselves from shame.

Expectation of being perfect

Shame also spreads its toxic poison when a child makes mistakes and causes upset or distress to another and is not led through the long but important process of identifying the feelings of guilt, sadness and embarrassment so that they can then be taught how to try to repair the mess. When this doesn't happen in the context of a warm and empathetic primary caregiver, the child can become a perfectionist or do anything to avoid mistakes or failure in case those deep self-rejecting feelings of shame surface and feel too big to cope with.

> Thus it is that an individual already burdened by a deep, abiding sense of defectiveness will strive to erase every blemish of the self and experiences of inordinate pressure to excel. (Kaufman 1980, p.90)

If the parent struggles with feelings of fear about failure and imperfection and is nervous that the child's imperfections/natural childlikeness may 'let them down' and hurt their well carved out reputation, this can lead to the parent exerting control over the child to such an extent that the child feels powerless, submissive and shamed.

Confusing boundaries

Shame can take root when the primary caregiver either feels shame about their humanity or they have no boundaries around letting the child see their raw humanity. When the child is cared for by an adult who doesn't have clear boundaries around what they wear, what they say and what they do and what they keep private, the child can end up feeling awkward and shame can begin to breed. When the child feels safe enough to talk about their concerns, then shame can't take root, unless they are told off for challenging and questioning their parent's boundaries.

Adolescence

We all recognize the challenges that come with adolescence and we know that when the child is affirmed and encouraged in this period of time they can grow up with confidence and navigate the ups and downs that hormones seem to facilitate. One of the boundaries regarding adolescence, however, is ensuring that any teasing, mocking, noticing or commenting on the person's changing body is stopped, because discomfort can turn to shame quickly if they have insecurity or early shame experiences. Young people often want to hide their physical changes but as this is almost impossible it can lead to them being easily shamed when they don't feel protected by loving, caring, respectful adults who stop intentional shaming.

School systems that shame children

Schools are developing their awareness of mental health issues and most are expressing a desire to care for the whole child. However, there are still practices that take place in schools where children are shamed.

Some schools think that having children wait outside the Head's office where other children walk past and can laugh at them is an effective way of curtailing their negative behaviour. Others put labels around their necks, or make them stand up in class to explain why they haven't done something. I am passionate about helping teachers always think about the context of a child and to recognize that often things are not all that they seem. This is an essential prerequisite before deciding on any consequences arising from a child not meeting expectations.

For example, too many children who don't bring their lunch, pen, books, homework or other important kit into school are then shamed and punished, when actually it was a miracle that they managed to get to school, because their home was chaotic and they were terrified, or they were alone, or they were caring for adults in some capacity. We need to always try to enable children to have an adult with whom they feel safe enough to talk through some of the challenges they are facing, who can then advocate for them with other staff and help them manage any unrealistic demands of school. Every staff member needs to be taught to begin to think about challenging behaviour by first asking themselves, 'I wonder what happened to them to cause this behaviour?'

It is also worth noting that 'every social and educational opportunity also provides the possibility of failure, children with core shame often struggle to participate in class, interact with peers, and feel like a part of the group' (Cozolino 2016, p.124).

This story was sent to me while I was in the process of writing this book:

My daughter is five years old. Her teacher disliked the way she yawned loudly in class so she told my daughter to stand at the front then asked all the children in the class to yawn loudly and then asked the children why they thought my daughter was so disruptive.

On a separate occasion the same teacher sat my daughter in the corridor for crying when she missed me, saying she was silly and telling the workman who were fixing the roof, 'I've got a headache from this one.' My daughter was repeatedly moved down the behaviour chart for going to the bathroom – at the school the children have to move themselves down (a name tag) in front of everybody else.

This led to a urine infection and this behaviour resulted in a very anxious, nervous and angry child. I am happy to say she is now absolutely fine; she had the most amazing role model of a teacher that had a great relationship with her the following year.

Religious influence

Some religious groups use shame to enforce conformity in behaviour and thinking. This is powerful and it can be tragic to see the efforts made by, and consequences for, those who want to belong to the group but can't or don't feel that they want to conform to these expectations.

Children tend to do what they see modelled by adults and often don't question it, so it's important to model reflection, questions and thinking together about expectations of any organization. Sometimes adults subconsciously relate to the leader of a religious group as if they are actually a small child themselves, and the leader is the parent, and therefore they are dependent on them for survival. They respond to the leader's expectations with submission because they are scared to be alone and lose their sense of belonging to the group and can therefore forget that they are adults who can make choices; instead they feel intimidated and fearful and can display other threat responses. Obviously, like schools, many religious organizations are committed to making sure that they work hard to protect the vulnerability of the group members, but an understanding of shame can empower people to reflect and make good choices.

Reflection points

- How can we help to build communities that don't use shame to harm?

- Which do you or your child struggle with the most: admitting you have a need, being compared, online pressure, secrecy, perfectionism or confusing boundaries?

- How is shame experienced at different ages?

Chapter 5

SHAME SYMPTOMS: WHEN CHILDREN WITHDRAW

Running away, hiding or becoming silent

The flight response, which is part of the physiological response to feelings of threat, can make us want to hide and run away. Shame causes us to want to hide, because it is a relational response to fear of rejection. This can mean that people who struggle with shame end up avoiding the terrible feeling by becoming isolated and not experiencing any emotional connection with anyone, which in turn can add to their shame and escalate other symptoms of shame. Some become silent to avoid the potential rejection, failure, confusion and nervousness around relational interactions. This can cause frustration which can then further their inability to have the courage to speak. Some children can become afraid to assert opinions or express feelings in any way as they already feel rejected and unwanted, or they may continually demand to be listened to so that they feel a sense of being valued. Shame can make a child focus on not being seen, being silent, secretive and alone so that the risks of rejection and further shaming are reduced. Sadly though, this also means that the opportunities for positive relational experiences are reduced, leading to further shame and disconnection and isolation.

Loneliness and withdrawing emotionally

Children can play with each other and yet can still feel deeply lonely because they don't feel known and this too can breed shame. It can make them think it's their fault that they are not known and make them withdraw further. As Brené Brown says, 'disengagement triggers shame and our greatest fears of being abandoned, unworthy and unlovable' (2012, p.52).

It can sometimes feel painfully lonely to be around people who are not emotionally connected with you. When the child withdraws due to the fear of shame, their feelings of worthlessness and sadness only increase and they find themselves in the shame cycle.

When they are forced to be sociable they can find themselves being compliant or people-pleasing to avoid rejection, or they can become anxious and take on different masks to cope with the fear. Sometimes people speak of those children who are like chameleons because they fit in with whatever setting they find themselves in to avoid rejection.

Apologizing continually

Many of us have been taught to say sorry for anything where we might be an inconvenience or when the person we may have disturbed looks unhappy. Some children, however, can end up saying sorry for everything continually and apologizing not just for any mistakes, but also for any perceived mistakes or perceived rejection or failure. They need to learn to be kind to themselves and not apologize to the world for their existence. Sometimes children say sorry all the time because they feel in their subconscious, or they have been told, that they are a disappointment. They can heal from the shame in the context of a warm and loving relationship where the child begins to sense that they have value and where they can explore their subconscious feelings of worthlessness.

My four children and I were at the library when my six-year-old needed the toilet. I asked the librarians if they had a toilet that he could use. They looked in horror, pointing to my son, asking if it was for him. Their faces looked disgusted at him for having such a need and immediately I felt sick and tight-chested as I realized I was being shamed for being a 'bad mum' and for having a son who had a natural need. I almost found myself apologizing profusely for him having to go, but felt that was ridiculous as it is a natural human need we all share! I made sure I talked my son through how silly it was that the librarians were so shocked and we wondered together if they ever used the toilet.

Wearing masks

Some children and young people adopt 'masks' as a way of coping with their sense of vulnerability, and almost pretend to be someone else so that they can experience acceptance and belonging. They can be one character in one setting and another one in another, as long as their needs are met. Peer pressure can be damaging for children who have a sense of worthlessness or shame as they can compromise their sense of uniqueness to experience being loved and belonging. Keeping up their facades can be exhausting and 'accounts for the lack of spontaneity in thinking and behaviour which limits the ability to take positive risks and reinforces the sense of helplessness and feeling trapped in the cycle of shame' (Sanderson 2015, p.66).

These responses can further lead to behaviours such as:

- finding it hard to make decisions or exert an opinion in case they get it wrong or are rejected

- having few friends or being controlling over a few friends

- not being vulnerable or honest about their feelings

- feeling powerless and embarrassed and so avoiding or being controlling in situations where they are 'seen'

- being people-pleasing to avoid criticism and rejection

- creating an identity that is a bad person so people won't try and be close to them.

When a child can discharge their feelings of shame with a caring adult who doesn't judge or want quick fixes, they can get a release from the cycle of shame, destructive behaviours and feelings that otherwise get trapped in the depth of their subconscious.

Compliance and fear of risk-taking

To avoid the feeling of shame, some children and young people will be compliant in their behaviour and do everything under the shadow of the terror of being 'told off' by any adult. They may well be too fearful to speak out about any personal opinion or even to be noticed in case they have got something wrong. Compliance is usually a sign that the child is too terrified to explore boundaries in relationships and instead lives in fear of causing things to 'get even worse' if they do anything that is seen as not fully conforming.

In a study of footballers (Sagar, Busch and Jowett 2010), the most common fear was the fear of shame and embarrassment. It is this fear that can stop those playing sports from taking risks and instead choose to play it safe to avoid any possible blame, shame and embarrassment. The thought of their team-mates focusing on their mistake, maybe the crowds shouting accusations, and having to live with the memory of their public mistake and subsequent shame can be too frightening. Children and young people see what happens when public figures are shamed and can be impacted in their confidence to take risks and instead can choose to stay safe and avoid any risks.

Reflection points

- Have you been aware of children who have responded like this? What did they need that they weren't able to put into words?

- How do you usually respond when children are 'loners', withdraw or pretend to be someone they are not?

- How will that change now?

Chapter 6

SHAME SYMPTOMS: WHEN CHILDREN DECEIVE OR BLAME

Lying

Shame can often cause children to lie to protect their vulnerability and fear of rejection. The lies serve to protect the child or young person from having to face the deep and intense feelings of shame that can trigger feelings of self-hatred and self-rejection. The child can lie so convincingly that they believe the lie themselves, as a desperate attempt to protect themselves from shame.

The way to respond as an adult is with love and empathy, either ignoring it for a while or reaching out gently and slowly with an empathetic response, such as telling a story of when you were young and lied because you were scared. The important thing is that they need you to wait patiently rather than challenging them in a confrontational way, because the experience becomes full of fear and they need love and nurture to be able to tell the truth and risk being vulnerable to the power you hold as an adult to hurt them.

Deceit

Deceit is a similar way of coping and is also often used as a way to protect vulnerability. When children are scared of showing who they are and 'being found out' or exposed, or being rejected, they aim subconsciously to deceive others. Lying is usually a simple untruth and deception is the consequence of lies as it builds a fuller picture that they want the people around them to believe because they feel like it will protect them. Deceit can be a subconscious survival mechanism to protect the person from having to face the reality of their lives, needs, issues and pains. This means that they will not realize they are using deceit at all, because they have convinced themselves it is true in order to hide their shame. All the tangled webs of lying and deceit can be slowly untangled when love, care and nurturing relationships help the person feel that being honest will be met with understanding and empathy within the relationship, rather than the loss of relationship.

Being critical of others and projection

When they are attempting to avoid experiencing or trying to cope with the weighty, dark feeling of shame, a child can subconsciously learn to be critical of others to dilute the pain. It is a way of deflecting the pain of self-hatred and the turmoil of feeling worthless and unlovable. If the person gets a sense of relief by being critical of others, it can develop into 'projection'. This is a subconscious coping mechanism to enable an overwhelmed person to manage their escalating feelings of self-hatred and shame. When they feel ashamed of something they have done they can project everything they hate about themselves onto other people and then become critical of them and gather others to agree with them against the other person. This can be hugely damaging to the person they are projecting onto and to themselves, as they live a life of confusion and distortion. They can try and cover up the self that they are rejecting so that it can never be exposed by 'weaving a web of intricate lies to such an extent that their very identity is a lie…with a sense so false that they may be seen as imposters' (Sanderson 2015, p.111).

Jenny was a 13-year-old who was popular and enjoyed taking 'selfies'. One day Samantha, who she thought was a friend, accused her on social media of lying about her end of junior school exam results and actually failing them all. Jenny found out that a group of girls had met and decided to ask everyone what she got for her results and, with lots of lies and laughter, soon the whole school thought *she* was a liar. The gossip soon spread that Jenny also broke up relationships and was a nasty, lying, stupid person. Maybe it won't surprise you to find out that, actually, Samantha had failed her exams and had seen several friends' relationships fail because of little lies she told and now felt such extreme shame that as she watched Jenny becoming more popular, she decided to do something to make sure no one ever found out the truth about *her*. What started as a single lie about Jenny grew into a web of deceit that led to Samantha feeling powerful because she was leading a gathering of girls who were voicing hatred to Jenny. This resulted in Jenny leaving school due to anxiety. A lie from someone protecting their feeling of shame and a bit of gossip with friends became a twisted story of projection and deceit that escalated in an attempt to protect Samantha's shame.

We need to create environments and communities that focus on being kind, empathetic and honest, in which we understand that people can behave in complex, instinctive ways when they feel threatened and that this can have long-term, disastrous consequences.

This doesn't mean that people who act this way are bad people, but that they are hurt and can hurt others in order to defend themselves. Gossip always hurts and is often based on someone's insecurity and need to defend themselves, which often stems from projection and deceit.

Reflection points

- How have I responded when a child has lied to me?

- How have I responded when a child has been deceitful, projected onto me or lied to me (rather than just lied)?

Chapter 7

SHAME SYMPTOMS: WHEN CHILDREN HATE THEMSELVES

The repeated experience of shame can cause children, young people and adults to subconsciously or consciously reject themselves. This can be obvious if the child makes statements like 'I'm useless, no one loves me', 'I can't make friends, everyone hates me', 'I'm ugly and stupid.' However, many children don't speak their shame words out loud; they echo in their minds and hearts instead.

Sadly, children can allow the shame to not just be a subconscious challenge but also a conscious decision to fuel their anger towards themselves, with self-criticism and self-aggression and self-disgust being normal internal self-talk (internal beliefs about themselves).

They can reject themselves by trying to act like someone they're not to fit in better and so have their need to belong met, or by taking 'selfies' that have fewer and fewer imperfections and increasing layers of make-up or filters. They can sabotage situations where they do feel happy and feel a sense of belonging because they don't ultimately feel that they deserve it.

One of the most helpful things we can do as caring adults is to develop relationships with these children and young people where we demonstrate care and respect consistently and show that we value the child. Then the words of affirmation that we give them can slowly dilute the negative self-talk and self-hatred. It can take time to rewire the brain of a person who has a history of feeling that they can't ever quite be enough or of worth, but it can be done!

Anger

Anger is a self-defensive emotion, but is not a 'bad emotion' that should be pushed down and 'managed'. It functions by 'insulating the self against further exposure and by actively keeping others away to avoid further occurrences of shame' (Kaufman 1980, p.17). It helps the child know when someone is doing something that feels wrong. How they then express the anger becomes a choice once it's acknowledged and welcomed as a helpful indication that something is not right. There is a great deal of shame about feeling angry, because adults often tell children to stop feeling anger and ironically can be harsh and angry in their attempts to stop the expression of anger. Children need to learn that anger is 'something that could be understood and handled, something that was even worthwhile and useful…' (Silberg 2013, p.152). When anger is pushed down, denied and covered in the shame of existing, it can be volcanic and explosive and aimed at everyone else whilst actually, below the words that are thrown around at others, huge self-hatred can lurk. Sometimes the self-hatred causes the child to be silent, withdrawn and lacking in confidence and at other times the self-hatred is projected onto others and they seem to hate everyone, even the most loving of adults who is trying to help them.

Self-destructive behaviours

Another way to cope with the feelings of self-hatred and self-rejection is to self harm. The experience generally produces a sense of comfort when the person inflicts pain on themselves. This is partly due to the endorphins that are released, which have a drug-like effect, and sadly there can also be comfort in the familiarity of feelings of pain.

Sabotaging relationships is also typical self-destructive behaviour that is due to the person's deeply enmeshed feelings of shame that they are unlovable and not worthy of respect, care, nurture and love.

Addictions can often begin in childhood as ways to self-soothe the inner turmoil and shame that hasn't been processed or made sense of. Obviously these early comfort-seeking behaviours can become lifelong dependencies which can be life-destroying. Early addiction can be things such as self-soothing behaviours, sugar, comforting food or fast stimuli such as screen time.

Brené Brown explains how shame can lead to self-destructive or other behaviours:

> When we experience shame, we feel disconnected and desperate for worthiness. When we're hurting either full of shame or even just the feeling of the fear of shame, we are more likely to engage in self destructive behaviours and to attack or shame others. (Brown 2012, p.73)

Again, the way to help the child is through understanding, empathy, kindness and emotional connection, fun, and laughter; eventually the brain rewires and healing can take place in the subconscious levels where the hidden shame lies.

Jason had been abused by his uncle since he was four years old and had been told that if he told anyone about the abuse, his dog would be killed. He lived with the secret, terrified of anyone finding out and losing his dog. His uncle liked to hang around the family home and tell his sisters that their brother was dating multiple girls, making up stories about what he got up to. The disgust that Jason felt led him to harbour deep feelings of self-loathing and anger. He would do anything to not live the life that he felt trapped within but blamed himself that he was too weak to escape and too afraid to fight. The shame kept him silent, scared and hating himself.

Reflection points

- Which of these behaviours have you seen in children and young people?

- How have you responded before?

- Now you can see some of the reasons behind the behaviours, will it help?

Chapter 8

SHAME SYMPTOMS: WHEN CHILDREN SHUT DOWN OR DISSOCIATE

Emotional shut-down

When a child, young person or adult feels 'emotionally too full', they can be left with little choice but to shut down their feelings. This means that as well as the negative feelings that they don't want to feel, they are unable to experience joy or happiness. There are so many consequences of shutting down emotion and these include the negative impact on their immune system and their nervous system, which can lead to physical illness.

Fisher (n.d.) explores how some families are anxious about emotional expression and so their children are taught implicitly that expressing emotions show that they are weak. This can lead to them shutting down their emotions due to overwhelm and confusion and fear of rejection. Fisher says that shame 'can act as a wall to all other emotions because you were taught that emotions make you weak and you feel shame for feeling emotions. Emotions were humiliating or dangerous. This is held in the subconscious memory system' (n.d.).

'Look, mummy!' says Rory, reaching up to hold her hand. He drags her to see the sitting room wall where he has made a pattern with pens and squashed food. He looks up, expecting to see his mum's delight with his creative expression, but is greeted with screams, tears and a look of horror and panic. With tears running down her face, Mum runs to the kitchen to get kitchen towels while shouting, 'Why did you do this to me. You cause nothing but problems. You just want to make me upset because you hate me.' Rory's delighted face has dropped and he sits frozen underneath the table. He is crying, wondering what has happened to his world. Now he is struggling with the fears of abandonment, rejection and being unlovable and alone. No one comes to comfort him and so slowly he moves away from others and shuts down his feelings.

_____

Dissociation

Dissociation was described in Chapter 3 (page 46) and is a part of the freeze response to threat. Many children and young people who are harmed are left with an overriding sense that they didn't do enough to stop the harm being done and so they blame themselves and feel shame for their 'weakness'. The experience of shame can also be so overwhelming that they then have to dissociate from it 'to defend against overwhelming emotions that cannot be processed' (Sanderson 2015, p.43). It also means that the child can remain in the relationship with the person who hurt them because they have pushed the experience out of conscious awareness, along with the feelings of shame and fear.

One study shows that up to 37% of rape victims go into freeze mode, which actually leads to increased self blame and increased post traumatic stress symptoms when the attack is over. (Galliono *et al.* 1993, quoted in Silberg 2013, p.129)

Freezing can be a short-term reaction, but it can also develop into a complex dissociative internal response. This is an instinctive, subconscious coping mechanism that will also become counterproductive because the child cannot choose when to stay in the here-and-now and when to dissociate or shut down different aspects of themselves.

Addiction

When the pain of shame or the exhaustion of the coping mechanisms used to avoid it become too much, sometimes the only thing left is to numb the pain. Every person is different with what they find that numbs their pain. In teenagers we see behaviours such as an extreme drive to win in sports, starving themselves, being popular, being a perfectionist, high adrenaline activities, parties or learning. In children, as we have mentioned before, we see other addictions such as demanding sugary food, new toys, constant stimuli, etc. As adults we often continue to develop these addictions to continue to numb the pain from internal, unresolved shame. Essentially, whatever enables the person to get a relief from the strong feelings and painful internal chaos of shame can become an addiction. Usually addictions mean that the child wasn't able to learn to comfort themselves using self-regulation and self-soothing, but instead relied on external help to soothe or escape the powerful feelings of shame and internal pain. As with many shame symptoms and behaviours, the person often then feels shame about the addictions, which can produce further emotions that need numbing. We need to be a society that stops asking 'Why the addiction?'; instead we must ask 'Why the pain?' because addiction is trying to soothe deep, unmet pain.

> We all have shame. We all have good and bad, dark and light, inside of us. But if we don't come to terms with our shame, our struggles, we start believing that there is something wrong with us – that we're bad, that we're flawed, not good enough – and even worse, we start acting on those beliefs. (Brown 2012, p.61)

Reflection points

- Have you seen these behaviours in children or young people? How have you responded to them?

- How can we create emotional safety to help those who have to shut down in some way feel able to feel again?

Chapter 9

OVERCOMING SHAME

The first four chapters explored the definition, context, impact and science of shame. The following four chapters explored some of the different conscious and subconscious ways children, young people and adults cope with the extremely uncomfortable feelings of shame. The final two chapters will explore how we can both heal from shame and build a shame-resilient culture – whether it is within a home, school, institution or broader community.

We have established that shame is first experienced as an interpersonal fear of being abandoned, rejected and not being good enough. This early childhood experience is either explored, expressed and validated or becomes internalized and subconscious. Conscious, spoken-about shame experiences rarely cause any subconscious behaviour changes or internal wounds, and short bursts of shame followed by healthy relational repair can strengthen the pro-social skills needed to create positive communities.

Provide healing emotional connection with the child

When adults are focused on helping children become healthy, we can become their helpers to stop the shame becoming embedded in their subconscious. When we can be empathetic, kind, non-judgemental, consistent and predictable adults, and use gentle affirming tones of voice, we can enable the child to feel safe enough to reflect on their behaviours and feelings.

We can reframe any toxic shame (Type II–III shame) as we reflect on it, so that the child can see it was a clever mechanism to enable them to stay alive and or stay in a painful dependent relationship with their carer for their needs to be met. Shame served them well for a period of time as a coping mechanism, but as they reflect and can see the further impact of it, this should enable them to slowly unravel some of the complex developing behaviours.

Being empathetic doesn't mean that we have to have experienced exactly the same incident but empathy acts as 'as a ladder out of the shame hole' (Brown 2012, p.81) by letting the child know that shame is a normal human response and we all share the same hatred of it.

When the shame experiences can be repaired through the kindness and empathy of a parent or caring familiar adult, research suggests that it can actually help build their resilience.

When an adult can regularly emotionally engage with the child, they begin to get used to this sense of connection. When a child has not experienced this, they can feel abandoned and shame can breed on the feelings of loneliness and rejection. This can lead to withdrawing emotionally, a common experience for many people that is usually hidden by behaviours that mask it; for instance popular, busy children who seem to be well-liked and invited to all the parties can often be emotionally disengaged and hiding internally in shame. Emotional connection takes courage but makes a person feel alive and known, and being known by others is a need deep in the heart of a human.

Tips for emotional connection with a child or young person

- Find somewhere where they feel emotionally safe – their home or somewhere where they don't feel embarrassed or watched by peers.

- Make sure you think through your body posture. With young children, be on their eye level. Younger children prefer it if you kneel down or sit down and play with toys, whereas some older children and adolescents may feel uncomfortable looking at you as it may feel too intense, so focus on a shared task. That could be anything from building a LEGO® model, cooking, making something, colouring, mending a bike, gardening, shopping etc.

- Concentrate on being relaxed and calm because if you are anxious, they will sense it and want to please you or may be scared and nervous. Then enjoy the time with them so that you can naturally show empathy for their worries or hurts, show kindness and tell them how much you believe the best about them. Be encouraging about specific things they have achieved or chosen not to do. General encouragement such as 'You are so great' is nice but not as effective as specific encouragement such as 'You did so well to persist then instead of giving up. I'm really proud of you', or 'You know I noticed you walk away when that kid tried to tease/ hurt/poke/ laugh at you. That was amazing. Well done.'

- Make sure that they feel your genuine concern, empathy, patience and care with your words and the time you take to be with them and by making sure that your facial responses match your words! A grumpy face saying 'I care' is just confusing for them and an adult looking at the clock all the time makes the child feel like they are not important!

- When an adult helps a child feel emotionally connected and cared for their feelings of shame become less powerful and begin to decrease.

Understanding normal human behaviour

One of the most helpful starting points for anyone wanting to live free from the entanglements of shame-fuelled behaviours and coping mechanisms is psycho-education. Learning about the impact, science and 'how' of shame can reduce its power as you come to understand the extreme feelings of terror and the need to avoid it. That's why the bulk of this book explores the way shame impacts us so we can break the power of silence and darkness around it.

Procedural memory is the implicit memory that enables us to remember how to do things automatically without conscious thinking, such as riding a bike, playing an instrument, swimming, etc. Understanding procedural memory can help a child or young person see how they behave and why they sometimes don't feel like they can control their shame and fear responses. When the child becomes aware of their instinctive responses to strong feelings or fearful situations, they may begin to notice that sometimes they dissociate, run away, shut down, laugh, distract another person, project – whatever reaction is typical for them; these are all instinctive ways to respond. Responses can be relearned once they have been noticed, noticed again, and then again, reflected on, and then understood as useful coping mechanisms which they can now begin to override and slowly begin to stop and to think instead. Essentially, when a neural pathway is identified, a new neural pathway can be formed as an alternative.

Speak up for cultures of vulnerability and kindness

The antidote to shame is building cultures of empathy and honesty that enable people to be safe enough to be vulnerable. Emotional connection with others is the only way to develop a culture of safety that enables people to risk being vulnerable. Talking about the impact of shame reduces its power and brings it out into the open, thereby reducing the shame about shame that develops when it is kept hidden.

Help wake up the child's frontal lobes!

Reflection and learning about shame require action from the frontal lobes, which actually 'go offline' when the person is fearful or is feeling threatened. To enable the frontal lobes to be able to reflect on the feelings and sensations of shame is essential and so we need to help the children and young people become curious about their responses to different situations. Some questions we can ask gently, when the child is in a safe place to reflect and is able to be curious, are:

- When you talk about feeling shame, where do you feel the feeling in your body?

- When you speak about being rejected/alone/ unwanted, where do you feel that?

- What words do you have whirling in your mind that come with the feeling? ('No one wants me', 'I always screw things up', 'I'm useless.')

- Do you think those words are true or are they your fears?

- What words can I say that make you feel safer and stronger?

Self-compassion

A child also needs to learn self-compassion for their own humanity and neediness rather than shame and frustration. If they can hear the gentle, kind, empathetic voice of a caring adult repeatedly affirming and encouraging them, then they are more likely to internalize that voice and be kind to themselves. When they are surrounded by voices that speak of failure and needing to work harder and not be so irritating, then they can internalize those voices and find it hard to hear encouragement. We need children to be able to articulate their needs, feel no shame about them and then reflect on how they feel and what could meet those needs.

Reflection points

- How do you show the children in your world that you care and emotionally connect to them?

- What do you find difficult about emotionally connecting with a child? Is it the time it takes, the focus, the distractions, or does it feel unfamiliar?

Chapter 10

SHAME RESILIENCE AND HEALING

When children can emotionally connect with others they can feel known and secure. When they can't emotionally connect because they don't know how to due to lack of experience with their primary caregivers, they can feel lonely and afraid. If they can't emotionally connect due to subconscious or conscious fear of rejection, abandonment or being found out, they can develop complex coping mechanisms that limit their potential pain in relationships but also limit the level of trust and joy.

To emotionally connect with others takes vulnerability, and even to love another involves the risk of being rejected, yet it is a core aspect of being fully human and being healthy. When people have been hurt in a relationship, they need to heal in a relationship. We need to be 'vulnerability detectors' though, so that we detect quickly when a child or adult is being vulnerable with us and react with appropriate empathy and kindness. What could be normal chat to us could be courageous vulnerability for them. For some people who are testing out being vulnerable, these early attempts at sharing their thoughts or feelings can lead to either trust being built or to further withdrawal if their attempts are met with insensitivity.

Ten ways to promote healing from shame

To heal from shame and to stop shame becoming toxic in the lives of the children we care about, we can make sure we do these things:

- Help children and young people notice and identify shame and speak about the physical and emotional feelings that present. Also, with older children, we need to be able to explore verbally the toxicity of bad experiences when they are kept secret and hidden.

- Help children explore and reflect on how shame helped them stay alive in the moment – maybe it made them silent, they hid or they shut down briefly. Then consider how helpful it was then but explore how it can be a hindrance now.

- We need to intentionally choose to build cultures where relationships of emotional connection and emotional safety are available. We must aim for consistent kindness, empathy and care for each other so that people can talk about shame and vulnerability.

- As adults we need to learn to speak about our vulnerabilities, our feelings of insecurity and fears of rejection, so that we are modelling these deep fears as a normal part of being human.

- We need to help children identify shame symptoms that adults may present, so that children are not so shockingly impacted by projection, blaming, mocking or deceitful behaviours from them. They can then raise their concerns with someone they trust.

- We need to voice and speak about the power of shame and the toxicity of it remaining secret; we must build cultures that enable a united effort to reduce the secrecy and champion bravery.

- We need to speak about the shocking normalization of using shame in conversations to assert opinion in some social media. We need to continue to show our horror and shock so that children do not think it's normal behaviour.

- We need to make space to exercise self-compassion and move away from self-criticism as a norm.

- We also need to talk about pursuing relationships and a sense of belonging with others.

- We need to teach children how to respond to shame-based bullying with replies that aren't aggressive, but are relaxed. For example, when a child says to you, 'You're really short' then just say, 'Yes, I am and so I can move fast.' The shame is usually silenced and this stops the bullying.

Beware perfection!

We will not be perfect and will sometimes shout at a child or make a comment under our breath or need to escape to the toilet to breathe or feel like wailing when the children we care for are pushing our buttons or testing us or frustrating us. No one is perfect and faultless and any parent who seems perfect may well be emotionally shut down in some way and so actually is not able to model a full range of healthy emotional responses. Attachment theory would suggest that when babies occasionally get dysregulated and then soothed they experience the rupture and repair and this enables them to be stronger than those who were prevented from experiencing any kind of little pain or distress. Janine Fisher (n.d.) echoes this: 'so often we try and avoid the distress and avoid them being dysregulated but actually we can repair it and help co-regulate them which is an opportunity to build using rupture and repair'.

How to help when a child's behaviour shows shame-based coping mechanisms

- Let's make sure our language separates out problem behaviours from the children themselves. Children are not bad – the behaviours can be problematic, but the children are not.

- We need to help children know that negative emotions are normal and there are some good ways of expressing them that don't harm others or themselves.

- When they feel bad about themselves we need to help them not run away from that or project the bad feelings onto others, but instead reflect with a caring adult who can speak kindly about their core identity as precious despite any problematic behaviours.

- We need to help children when they make mistakes and help them know that they are normal. If we have hurt others by our mistakes then we can learn to try and put things right.

- We need to create environments that reflect on why someone is behaving in certain ways and assume that there is an unmet need there.

- When we praise them, they may find that difficult because they hold such a negative view of themselves. So praise the task briefly rather than generalizations such as, 'What a great kid.' Also, praise effort rather than achievement and let them express pleasure that may seem disproportionate.

Top tips on how to respond to a crying or angry child

If a child is crying it's always best to let them cry and make sure that they feel the empathy of the adults around them, even if what they are crying about seems to be so minor compared to the struggles adults face. When a child is crying or being cross it can be good to say things like:

- It's OK to cry
- It's OK to be sad/cross/frustrated
- I wonder if you felt scared/sad/unsure just then?
- I'm here if I can help
- Do you want to tell me about it?

- I'm here close by for when you are ready to let me help you

- I'm sorry that you feel so sad/cross/upset

- How can you communicate your sadness/irritation/frustration/annoyance/anger in a way that doesn't hurt you, others or the room?

Praising children for their good character, wise decisions and gifts

We need to make sure that we are speaking positive words to and about our children all the time. There are so many negative words, comparisons, strong media expectations and general nastiness and bullying on social media that we need to intentionally counteract this by using positive, affirming words. Children and young people need us to respect them and to know them. This takes time. As we learn to identify their character strengths, skills and talents and when they make good decisions, we need to praise them specifically. Encouragement and praise help shame to be repelled from children. We all need many more positive words spoken to counteract the negative ones and as we look for the gold in children we care for, rather than point out the mistakes and the weaknesses, they will grow in confidence and emotional strength and thus shame will have less power.

Conclusion

We also need to remember that our story is unfolding and hasn't ended yet, so there is always time to see change and find new freedom. 'Jung said, "I am not what happened to me. I am what I choose to become"' (Brown 2012, p.80).

Being human is a gift and being able to embrace all our humanity, vulnerability, longings, desires, hopes and dreams, and know that none of us is as simple as we seem, enables us to all play our part in building communities that celebrate our uniqueness and to believe the best about each other. Let's defend those who are being shamed and living with shame symptoms, and consistently show we care until they can trust and believe in themselves and others again.

Reflection points

- How can we help children to not connect their behaviour with their core identity?

- How can we help children explore negative emotions?

- What can I do to help children and young people be shame-resilient?

REFERENCES AND RECOMMENDED READING

References

Andrews, B. and Gilbert, P. (1998) *Shame: Interpersonal Behaviour, Psychopathology and Culture (Series in Affective Science)*. Oxford: Oxford University Press.

Brown, B. (2012) *Daring Greatly: How the Courage to Be Vulnerable Transforms the Way We Live, Love, Parent and Lead*. New York: Portfolio Penguin.

Cozolino, L. (2006) *The Neuroscience of Human Relationships. Attachment and the Developing Social Brain*. New York: W.W.Norton.

Cozolino, L. (2016) *Why Therapy Works. Using our Minds to Change Our Brains*. New York: W.W.Norton.

Fisher, J. (n.d.) Online Course: Complex Trauma and Shame: Somatic Interventions with Janina Fisher, PhD. Psychotherapy Excellence. Accessed 15/12/17 at www.psychotherapyexcellence.com

Gerhardt, S. (2004) *Why Love Matters. How Affection Shapes a Baby's Brain*. Hove: Brunner-Routledge.

Herman, J.L. (2011) 'Shattered Shame States and Their Repair.' In J. Yellin and K. White (eds): *Shattered States: Disorganised Attachment and its Repair*. London: Karnac.

Kaufman, G. (1980) *Shame: The Power of Caring*. Cambridge, MA: Schenkman Publishing.

Sagar. S., Busch, B. and Jowett, S. (2010) 'Success and failure, fear of failure, and coping responses of adolescent academy football players.' *Journal of Applied Sports Psychology 2*, 2, 213–230. Accessed on 18/6/18 at www.researchgate.net/publication/234092864_Success_and_Failure_Fear_of_Failure_and_Coping_Responses_of_Adolescent_Academy_Football_Players.

Sanderson, C. (2015) *Counselling Skills for Working with Shame.* London: Jessica Kingsley Publishers.

Schore, A. (2003) *Affect Regulation and the Repair of the Self.* (Norton Series on Interpersonal Neurobiology.) New York: W.W.Norton.

Silberg, J. (2013) *The Child Survivor. Healing Developmental Trauma and Dissociation.* New York: Routledge.

Recommended Reading

Brown, B. (2007) *I Thought It Was Just Me: Women Reclaiming Power and Courage in a Culture of Shame.* New York: Penguin Group.

Brown, B. (2012) *The Unspoken Epidemic of Shame.* Available at www.youtube.com/watch?v=psN1DORYYV0 (TED Talk), accessed on January 15, 2013.

de Thierry, B. (2015) *Teaching the Child on the Trauma Continuum.* Guildford: Grosvenor Publishing.

de Thierry, B. (2016) *The Simple Guide to Child Trauma.* London: Jessica Kingsley Publishers.

Levery. S. (2013) 'Let's learn together.' Accessed on 15/03/17 at www.adoptionuk.org/lets-learn-together-ni.

Van der Hart, O., Nijenhuis, E.R.S. and Steele, K. (2006) *The Haunted Self: Structural Dissociation and the Treatment of Chronic Traumatization.* New York: W.W.Norton.

INDEX

The Simple Guide to Child Trauma

Betsy de Thierry

Foreword by David Shemmings

Illustrated by Emma Reeves

£8.99 / $14.95

ISBN 978 1 78592 136 0

eISBN 978 1 78450 401 4

- What is trauma?
- How does it affect children?
- How can adults help?

Providing straightforward answers to these complex questions, *The Simple Guide to Child Trauma* is the perfect starting point for any adult caring for or working with a child who has experienced trauma. It will help them to understand more about a child's emotional and behavioural responses following trauma and provides welcome strategies to aid recovery. Reassuring advice will also rejuvenate adults' abilities to face the challenges of supporting children.

The Simple Guide to Sensitive Boys

Betsy de Thierry

Foreword by Jane Evans

Illustrated by Emma Reeves

£8.99 / $14.95

ISBN 978 1 78592 325 8

eISBN 978 1 78450 639 1

What do Pablo Picasso, Prince and Martin Luther King Jr have in common? All have been described as having been highly sensitive boys and all grew up to be outstanding, sensitive men.

Too often, adults think of sensitive boys as shy, anxious and inhibited. They are measured against society's ideas about 'manliness' – that all boys are sociable, resilient and have endless supplies of energy. This highly readable guide is for any adult wanting to know how to understand and celebrate sensitive boys. It describes how thinking about boys in such old-fashioned ways can cause great harm, and make a difficult childhood all the more painful. The book highlights the real strengths shared by many sensitive boys – of being compassionate, highly creative, thoughtful, fiercely intelligent and witty. It also flips common negative clichés about sensitive boys being shy, anxious and prone to bullying to ask instead: What we can do to create a supportive environment in which they will flourish?

Full of simple yet sage advice, this book will help you to encourage boys to embrace their individuality, find their own place in the world and to be the best they can be.

The Simple Guide to Attachment Difficulties in Children

Betsy de Thierry

Foreword by Carrie Grant
Illustrated by Emma Reeves

£9.99 / $14.95
ISBN 978 1 78592 639 6
eISBN 978 1 78592 640 2

- What are attachment difficulties?
- How do they affect children?
- How can you help

This book provides clear and concise answers to these important questions – and more.

Much more than just a simple introduction to the subject of attachment, the book is also full of advice and practical ideas you can try. It tackles some challenging questions, such as 'what is the difference between trauma and attachment?' and explains how having an understanding of attachment is only part of the overall picture when it comes to caring for traumatized children

It is an essential read for any adult parenting or caring for a child who has experienced attachment difficulties..